Introducing

Grunge Flower

TEXTURES VOL.1

I have a dualistic theory of style and art and this allows me to determine one style as opposed to another.
This book develops designs in the floral world with a particular imprint called GRUNGE in opposition to a synthetic, iconographic, linear, geometric vision.
I could represent the flowers in different ways with regular lines demarcating the contours and shadows as in FASHION FLOWER TEXTURES or in a highly geometric synthesis as in TECNO POP or lines convoluted, complex and repetitive as in BLACK & WHITE MATRIX 3.
In this volume instead I have created designs where the broken, smudged, sketchy sign is predominant and the backgrounds are irregular to the limit of abstraction.
In this gallery I have also included images with fresh strokes and watercolour stains because they express a touch of irregularity that is part of this new concept.

Indeed, expanding the initial concept of GRUNGE helps to find a common way of classifying a design within a larger family as opposed to the rational, tech, minimalist style prevailing in the world today.
But it is a dual world that opposes rational to irrational, regular to irregular, geometric to abstract, linear-precise to GRUNGE.
And both styles are now functional to our need of representation and our way of being contemporary.

Published by
ARKIVIA BOOKS srl

Via Provinciale , 68
24022 Alzano Lombardo
Bergamo (Italy)
Phone:
(0039) 035515851
web:
www.arkiviabooks.com
www.vincenzosguera.com
e-mail:
info@arkiviabooks.com
info@vincenzosguera.com

The DVD included is an integral part of this publication and cannot be sold separately.

Copyright and Rights to Use

DVD *info / Technical Details*

The Book contains a DVD suitable for WINDOWS® and MACINTOSH®

FORMAT
I have chosen the format JPG as files are very large, both in cm. and bites. If I used a PDF file, for example, it would need as many as 4 or 5 DVDs. I preferred a large size, near to their real use and a final resolution which is quite high and professional = 300 ppi. In addition to this folder (300 ppi CMYK) I have also added a folder with the same files at 72 ppi in RGB for easy reference.

Each of the two folders contains the same 165 designs but with a different resolution and different colour scale, 370 files in total. Here are the FOLDERS:

JPG 300 ppi - CMYK
These Files are in JPG Format saved at 300 ppi resolution and in CMYK.

JPG 72 ppi - RGB
Here you find Low Resolution BITMAP Files in JPG format (72 ppi in colour scale RGB), that can be used to develop projects with lighter Files and are for quick vision.

TYPE OF FILES
The Files in the DVD are all BITMAP: this means in the first place that they can be opened by all softwares that use BITMAP Format.

SOFTWARE
The main BITMAP software is: PHOTOSHOP but it is possible to open these files in software such as CORELPAINT, PAINTSHOP, COREL PAINTER etc.

SIZES
The size of the files is listed both in centimetres and in pixels at 300 ppi.

COLOURS
In BITMAP files the colours can be in RGB (Red, Green and Blue), more useful for video and internet use, or in CMYK (Cyan, Magenta, Yellow and Black) normally used for printing needs.

References

Some textures in this book are freely elaborated from designs which are in the following books:

1-FLOWER FASHION TEXTURES VOL.1 by Vincenzo Sguera / Rosangela Fiorella
2-GOTHIC POP TEXTURES VOL.1 by Vincenzo Sguera
3-GRAPHICOLLECTION-ARTWORK VOL.2 by Annalisa Gemmi
4-GRAPHICOLLECTION-MINI PATTERN VOL.1 by Annalisa Gemmi
5-NATURAL POP TEXTURES VOL.1 by Vincenzo Sguera
6-NATURAL POP TEXTURES VOL.2 by Vincenzo Sguera
7-SIMPLE NATURE TEXTURES VOL.1 by Vincenzo Sguera e Rosangela Fiorella
8-ULTRA POP TEXTURES VOL.2 by Vincenzo Sguera

GFT0001
pattern size
50 cm x 50 cm
5906 x 5906 pixels
at 300 ppi in CMYK

GFT0002
pattern size
50 cm x 50 cm
5906 x 5906 pixels
at 300 ppi in CMYK

GFT0003
pattern size
50 cm x 50 cm
5906 x 5906 pixels
at 300 ppi in CMYK

page 007 >>

GFT0005
pattern size
50 cm x 50 cm
5906 x 5906 pixels
at 300 ppi in CMYK

GFT0006
pattern size
42 cm x 44 cm
4961 x 5197 pixels
at 300 ppi in CMYK

GFT0004
pattern size
50 cm x 50 cm
5906 x 5906 pixels
at 300 ppi in CMYK

<< page 008

GFT0007
pattern size
35 cm x 50 cm
4134 x 5906 pixels
at 300 ppi in CMYK

GFT0008
pattern size
35 cm x 50 cm
4134 x 5906 pixels
at 300 ppi in CMYK

GFT0009
pattern size
60 cm x 42 cm
7087 x 4961 pixels
at 300 ppi in CMYK

page 011 >>

GFT0011
pattern size
40 cm x 40 cm
4724 x 4724 pixels
at 300 ppi in CMYK

GFT0012
pattern size
50 cm x 50 cm
5906 x 5906 pixels
at 300 ppi in CMYK

GFT0010
pattern size
50 cm x 58 cm
5906 x 6850 pixels
at 300 ppi in CMYK

<< page 012

GFT0013
pattern size
58 cm x 60 cm
6850 x 7087 pixels
at 300 ppi in CMYK

GFT0014
pattern size
50 cm x 50 cm
5906 x 5906 pixels
at 300 ppi in CMYK

GFT0015
pattern size
66 cm x 70 cm
7796 x 8263 pixels
at 300 ppi in CMYK

page 015 >>

<< page 016

GFT0016
pattern size
50 cm x 50 cm
5906 x 5906 pixels
at 300 ppi in CMYK

GFT0017
pattern size
50 cm x 50 cm
5906 x 5906 pixels
at 300 ppi in CMYK

page 018

GFT0018
pattern size
35 cm x 50 cm
4134 x 5906 pixels
at 300 ppi in CMYK

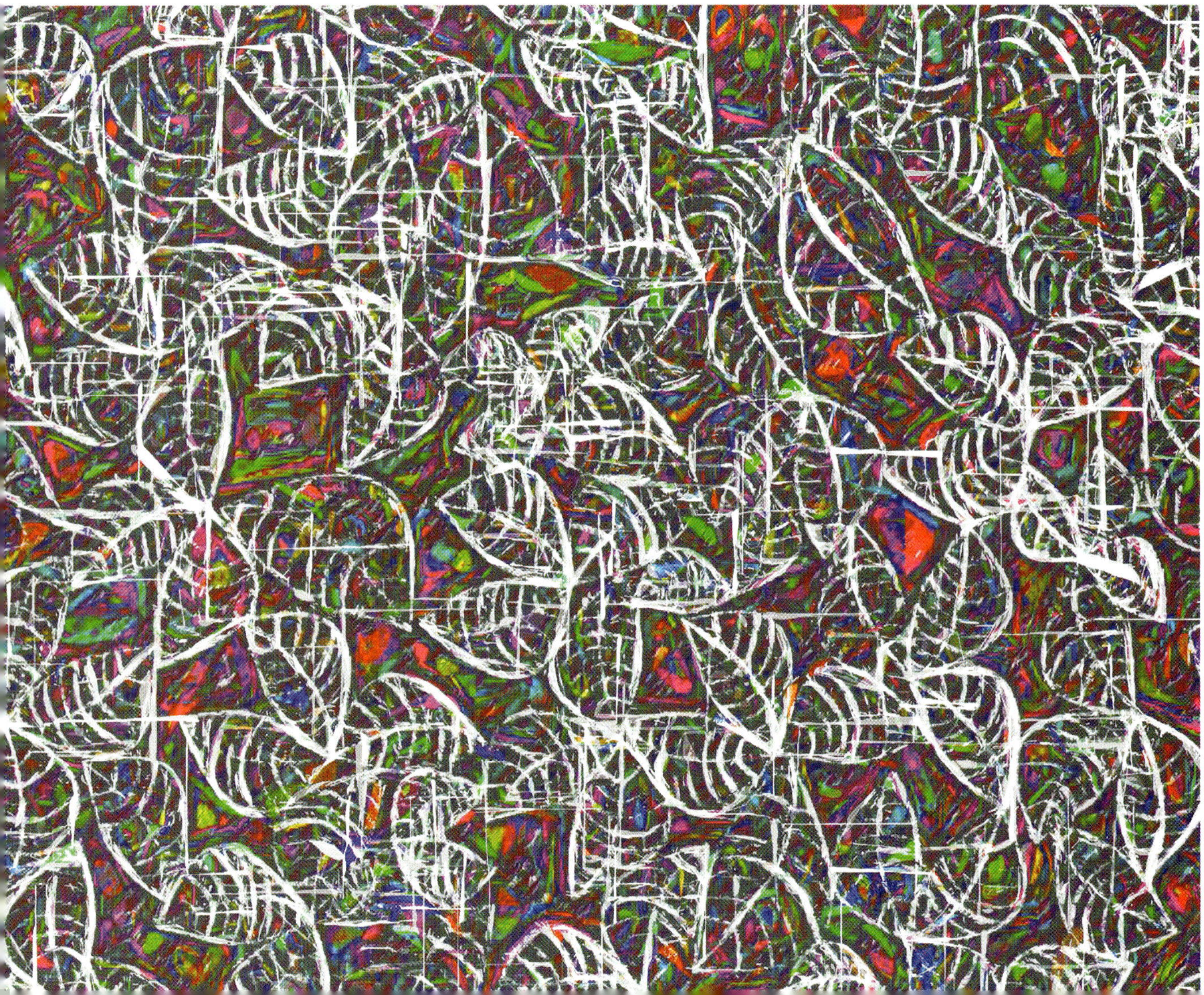

GFT0019
pattern size
50 cm x 50 cm
5906 x 5906 pixels
at 300 ppi in CMYK

GFT0020
pattern size
45 cm x 45 cm
5315 x 5315 pixels
at 300 ppi in CMYK

page 019 >>

GFT0022
pattern size
40 cm x 50 cm
4724 x 5906 pixels
at 300 ppi in CMYK

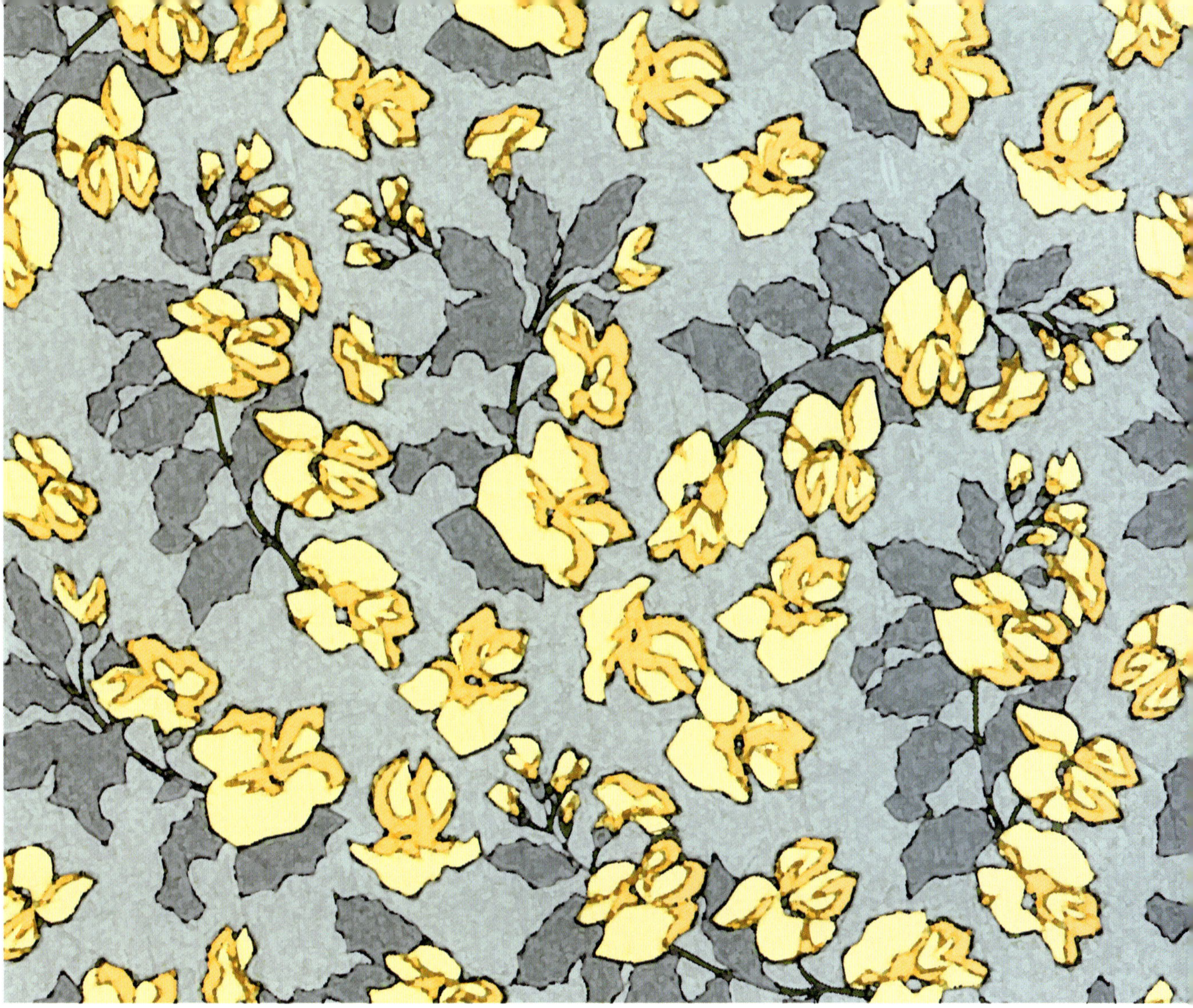

GFT0023
pattern size
40 cm x 50 cm
4724 x 5906 pixels
at 300 ppi in CMYK

GFT0021
pattern size
60 cm x 75 cm
7087 x 8859 pixels
at 300 ppi in CMYK

<< page 020

<< page 022

GFT0024
pattern size
40 cm x 40 cm
4724 x 4724 pixels
at 300 ppi in CMYK

GFT0025
pattern size
40 cm x 40 cm
4724 x 4724 pixels
at 300 ppi in CMYK

GFT0026
pattern size
40 cm x 40 cm
4724 x 4724 pixels
at 300 ppi in CMYK

GFT0027
pattern size
45 cm x 55 cm
5197 x 6496 pixels
at 300 ppi in CMYK

GFT0028
pattern size
40 cm x 52 cm
4724 x 6142 pixels
at 300 ppi in CMYK

GFT0029
pattern size
50 cm x 60 cm
5906 x 7087 pixels
at 300 ppi in CMYK

page 025 >>

<< page 026

GFT0030
pattern size
50 cm x 50 cm
5906 x 5906 pixels
at 300 ppi in CMYK

GFT0031
pattern size
46 cm x 44 cm
5434 x 5197 pixels
at 300 ppi in CMYK

GFT0032
pattern size
40 cm x 40 cm
4724 x 4724 pixels
at 300 ppi in CMYK

GFT0033
pattern size
40 cm x 40 cm
4724 x 4724 pixels
at 300 ppi in CMYK

GFT0034
pattern size
40 cm x 40 cm
4724 x 4724 pixels
at 300 ppi in CMYK

GFT0035
pattern size
40 cm x 40 cm
4724 x 4724 pixels
at 300 ppi in CMYK

page 029 >>

GFT0036
pattern size
30 cm x 50 cm
3543 x 5906 pixels
at 300 ppi in CMYK

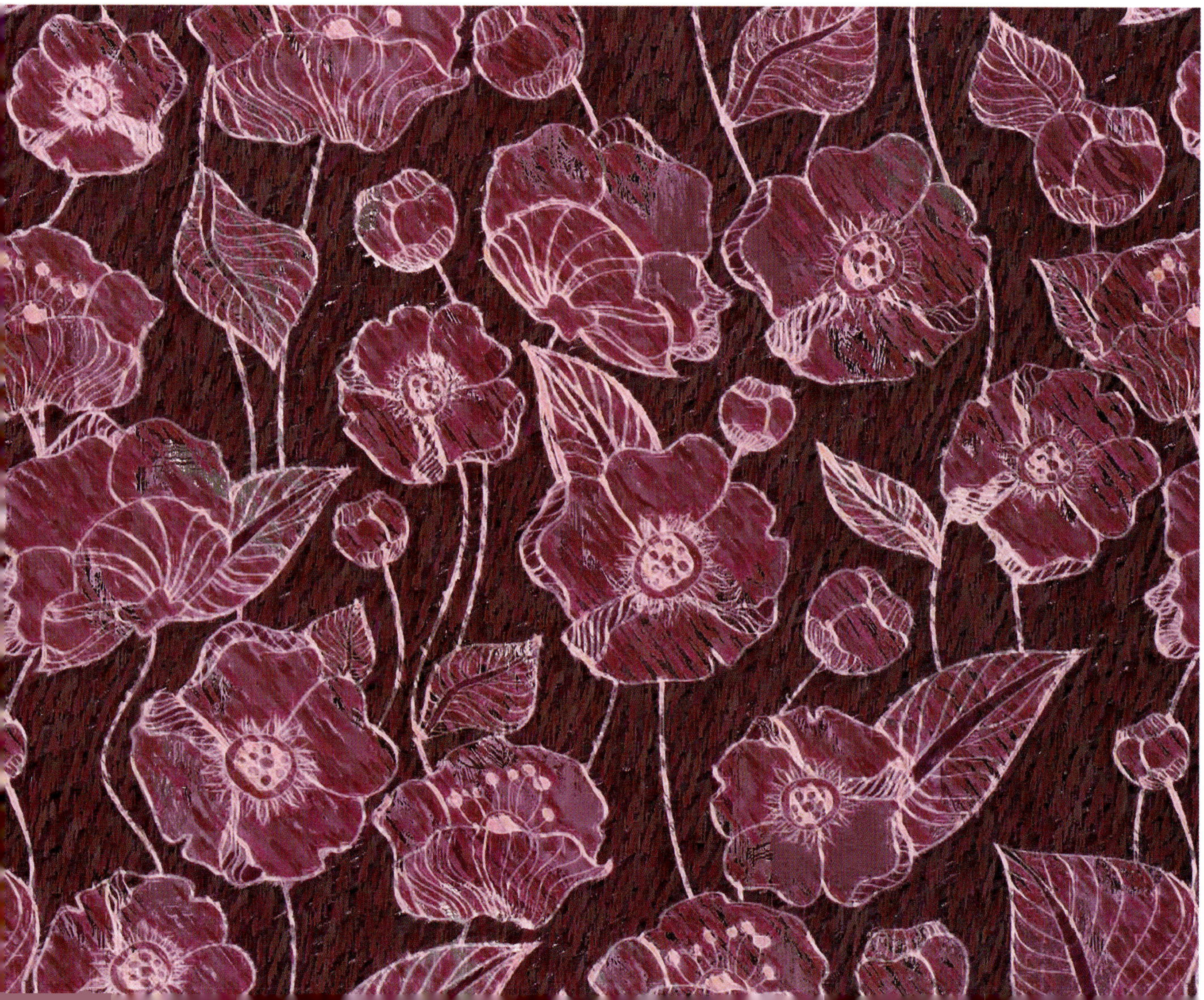

GFT0037
pattern size
30 cm x 50 cm
3543 x 5906 pixels
at 300 ppi in CMYK

GFT0038
pattern size
30 cm x 50 cm
3543 x 5906 pixels
at 300 ppi in CMYK

page 031 >>

<< page 032

GFT0039
pattern size
40 cm x 50 cm
4724 x 5906 pixels
at 300 ppi in CMYK

GFT0040
pattern size
50 cm x 50 cm
5906 x 5906 pixels
at 300 ppi in CMYK

GFT0041
pattern size
50 cm x 53 cm
5906 x 6260 pixels
at 300 ppi in CMYK

GFT0042
pattern size
25 cm x 60 cm
2953 x 7087 pixels
at 300 ppi in CMYK

GFT0043
pattern size
25 cm x 60 cm
2953 x 7087 pixels
at 300 ppi in CMYK

GFT0044
pattern size
60 cm x 43 cm
7087 x 5079 pixels
at 300 ppi in CMYK

page 035 >>

<< page 036

GFT0045
pattern size
50 cm x 53 cm
5906 x 6260 pixels
at 300 ppi in CMYK

GFT0046
pattern size
40 cm x 50 cm
4724 x 5960 pixels
at 300 ppi in CMYK

GFT0047
pattern size
60 cm x 55 cm
7087 x 6496 pixels
at 300 ppi in CMYK

GFT0048
pattern size
60 cm x 55 cm
7087 x 6496 pixels
at 300 ppi in CMYK

GFT0049
pattern size
74 cm x 50 cm
8741 x 5906 pixels
at 300 ppi in CMYK

page 039 >>

GFT0051
pattern size
40 cm x 60 cm
4724 x 7087 pixels
at 300 ppi in CMYK

GFT0052
pattern size
42 cm x 60 cm
4961 x 7087 pixels
at 300 ppi in CMYK

GFT0050
pattern size
50 cm x 50 cm
5906 x 5906 pixels
at 300 ppi in CMYK

<< page 040

<< page 042

GFT0053
pattern size
25 cm x 60 cm
2953 x 7087 pixels
at 300 ppi in CMYK

GFT0054
pattern size
25 cm x 60 cm
2953 x 7087 pixels
at 300 ppi in CMYK

GFT0055
pattern size
25 cm x 60 cm
2953 x 7087 pixels
at 300 ppi in CMYK

GFT0056
pattern size
52 cm x 40 cm
6142 x 4724 pixels
at 300 ppi in CMYK

GFT0057
pattern size
36 cm x 44 cm
4252 x 5197 pixels
at 300 ppi in CMYK

page 045 >>

<< page 046

GFT0058
pattern size
50 cm x 58 cm
5906 x 6850 pixels
at 300 ppi in CMYK

GFT0059
pattern size
60 cm x 54 cm
7087 x 6378 pixels
at 300 ppi in CMYK

GFT0060
pattern size
35 cm x 50 cm
4134 x 5906 pixels
at 300 ppi in CMYK

GFT0061
pattern size
45 cm x 60 cm
5315 x 7087 pixels
at 300 ppi in CMYK

GFT0062
pattern size
30 cm x 30 cm
3543 x 3543 pixels
at 300 ppi in CMYK

GFT0063
pattern size
30 cm x 30 cm
3543 x 3543 pixels
at 300 ppi in CMYK

GFT0064
pattern size
30 cm x 30 cm
3543 x 3543 pixels
at 300 ppi in CMYK

GFT0065
pattern size
30 cm x 30 cm
3543 x 3543 pixels
at 300 ppi in CMYK

page 049 >>

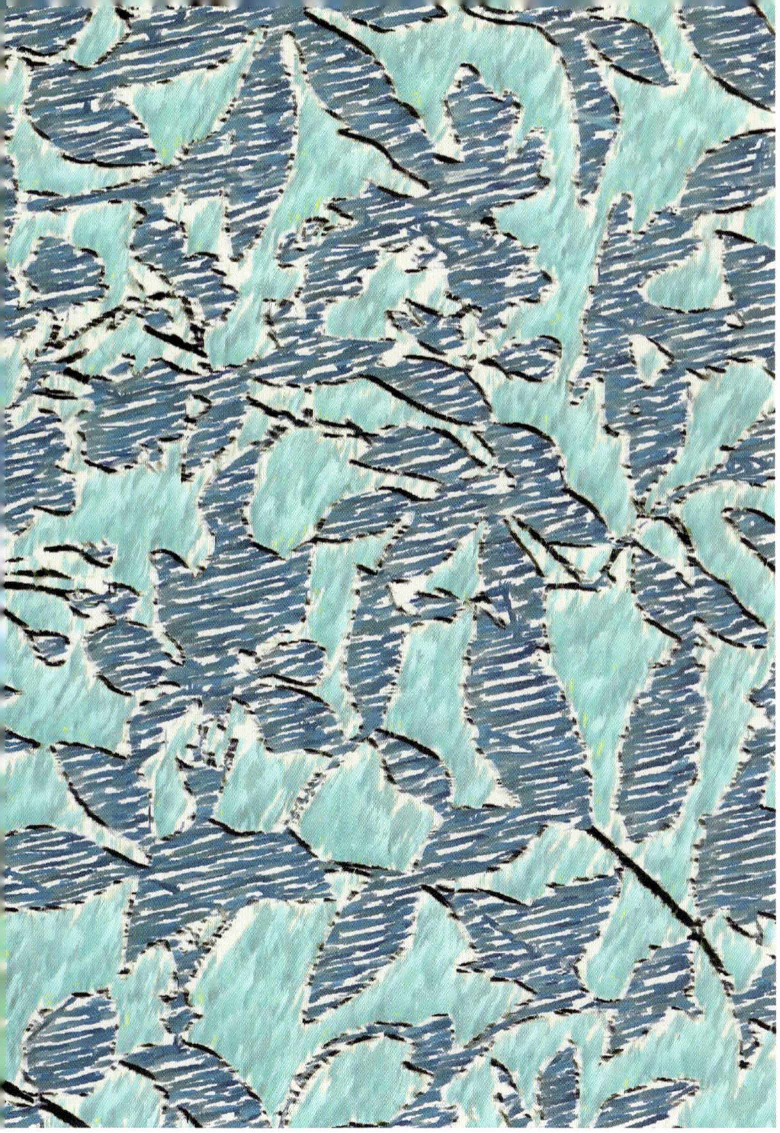
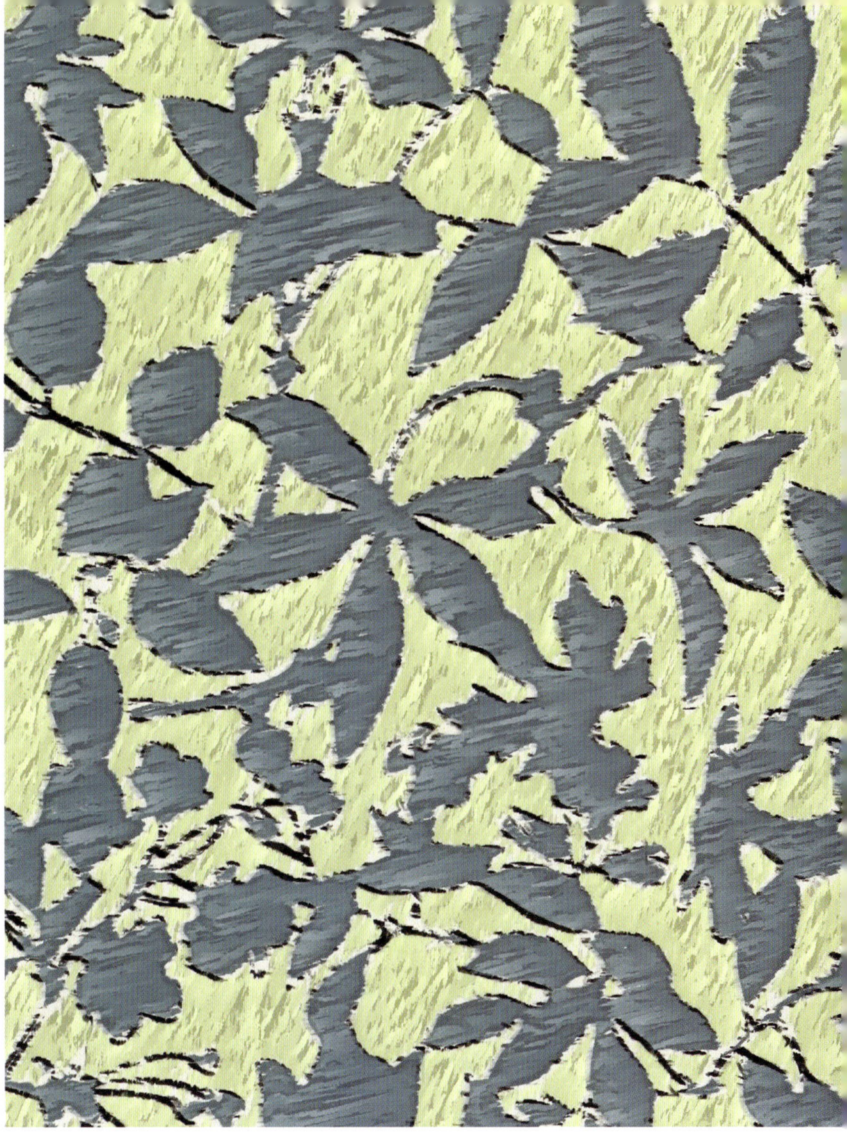

GFT0066
pattern size
64 cm x 70 cm
7559 x 8268 pixels
at 300 ppi in CMYK

GFT0067
pattern size
75 cm x 60 cm
8858 x 7087 pixels
at 300 ppi in CMYK

page 051 >>

<< page 052

GFT0068
pattern size
46 cm x 70 cm
5433 x 8268 pixels
at 300 ppi in CMYK

GFT0069
pattern size
64 cm x 70 cm
7559 x 8268 pixels
at 300 ppi in CMYK

GFT0070
pattern size
58 cm x 50 cm
6850 x 5906 pixels
at 300 ppi in CMYK

GFT0071
pattern size
64 cm x 70 cm
7559 x 8268 pixels
at 300 ppi in CMYK

GFT0072
pattern size
68 cm x 70 cm
8032 x 8268 pixels
at 300 ppi in CMYK

page 055 >>

GFT0074
pattern size
70 cm x 65 cm
8268 x 7678 pixels
at 300 ppi in CMYK

GFT0075
pattern size
70 cm x 65 cm
8268 x 7678 pixels
at 300 ppi in CMYK

GFT0073
pattern size
75 cm x 54 cm
8858 x 6378 pixels
at 300 ppi in CMYK

<< page 056

GFT0076
pattern size
50 cm x 62 cm
5906 x 7323 pixels
at 300 ppi in CMYK

GFT0077
pattern size
64 cm x 70 cm
7559 x 8268 pixels
at 300 ppi in CMYK

page 059 >>

<< page 060

GFT0078
pattern size
50 cm x 60 cm
5906 x 7087 pixels
at 300 ppi in CMYK

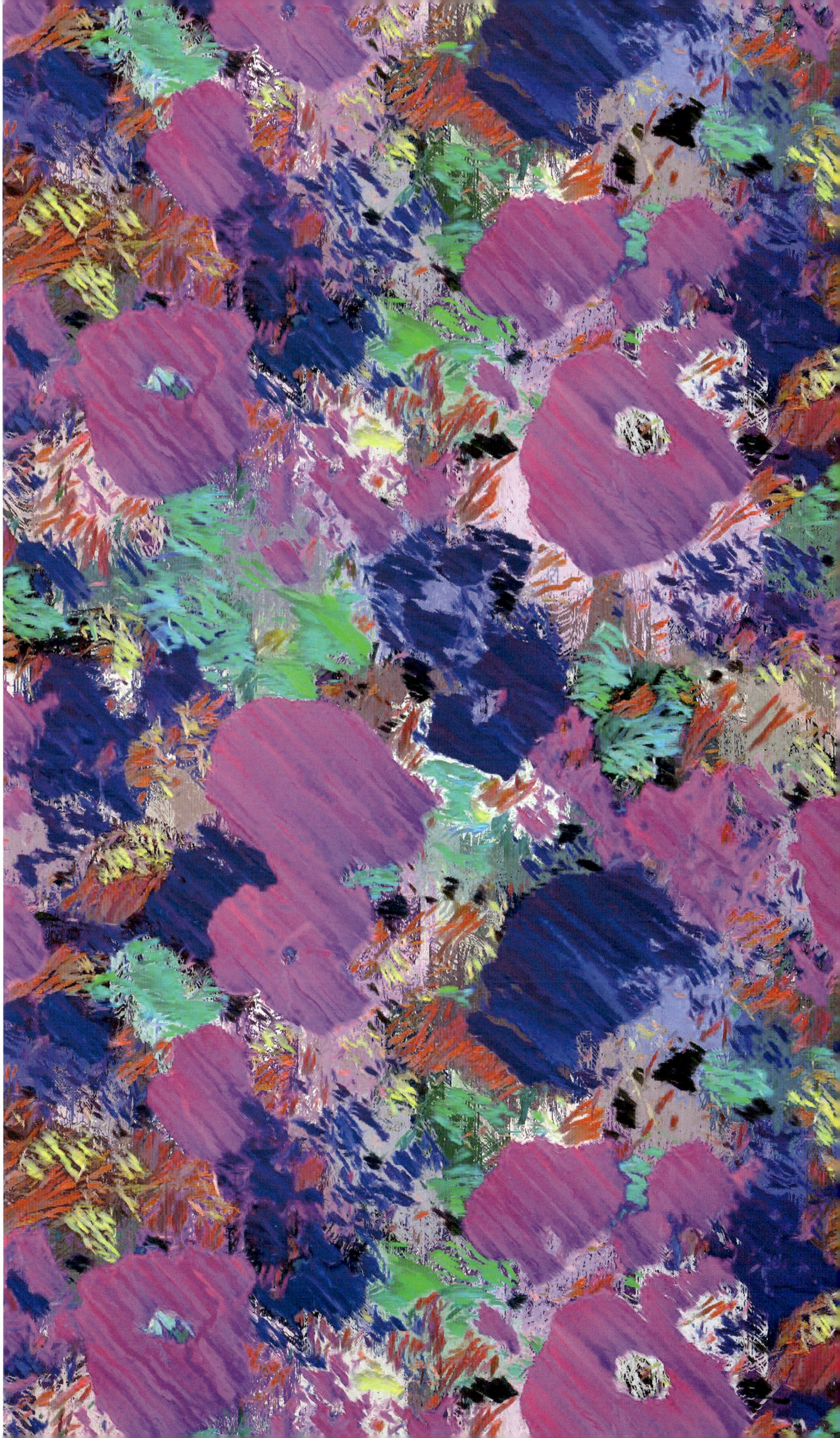

GFT0079
pattern size
70 cm x 45 cm
8268 x 5315 pixels
at 300 ppi in CMYK

page 061

GFT0080
pattern size
50 cm x 60 cm
5906 x 7087 pixels
at 300 ppi in CMYK

GFT0081
pattern size
75 cm x 60 cm
8858 x 7087 pixels
at 300 ppi in CMYK

page 063 >>

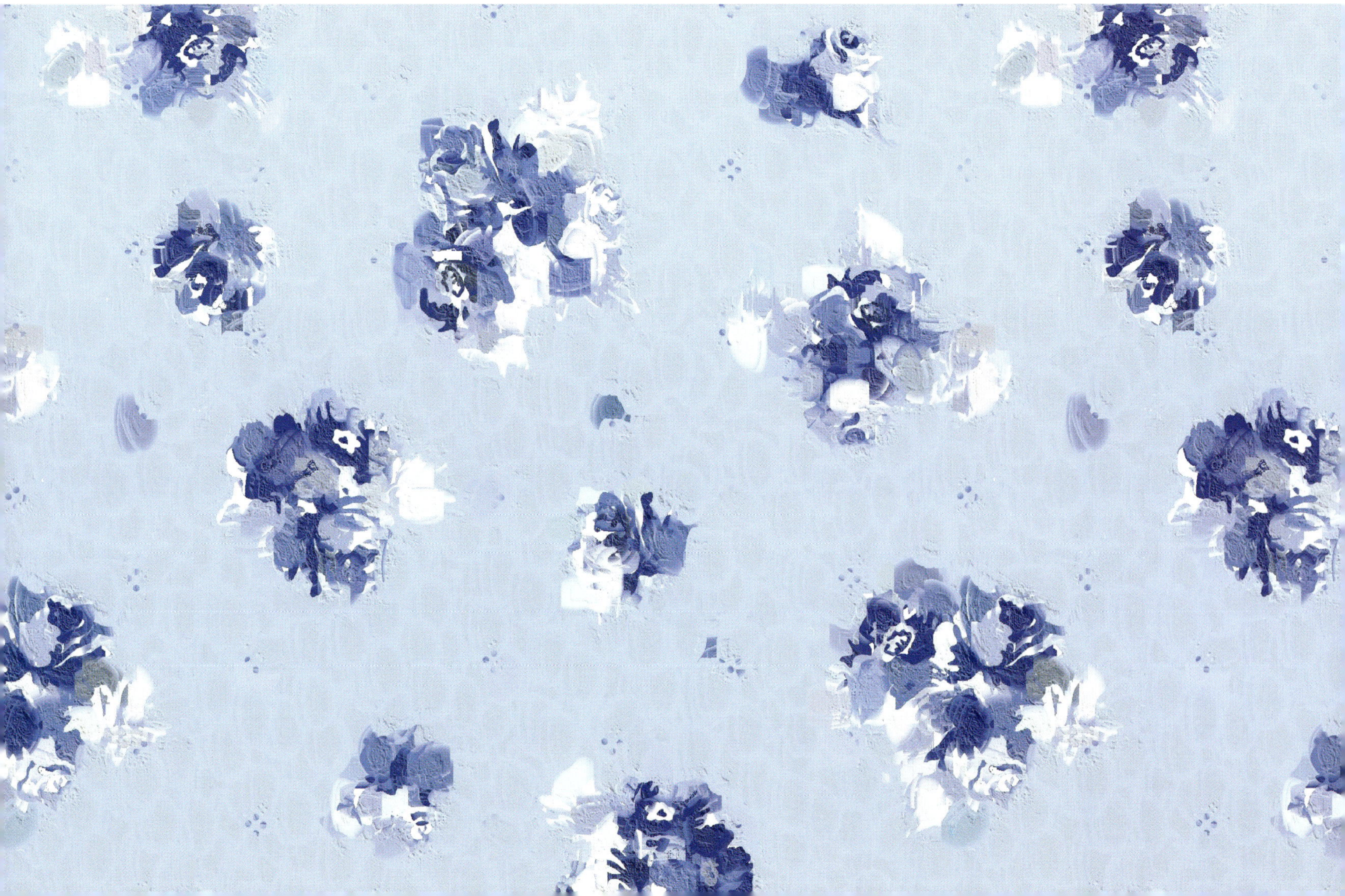

<< page 064

GFT0082
pattern size
60 cm x 60 cm
7087 x 7087 pixels
at 300 ppi in CMYK

GFT0083
pattern size
25 cm x 25 cm
2953 x 2953 pixels
at 300 ppi in CMYK

GFT0084
pattern size
50 cm x 50 cm
5906 x 5906 pixels
at 300 ppi in CMYK

GFT0085
pattern size
60 cm x 66 cm
7087 x 7795 pixels
at 300 ppi in CMYK

GFT0086
pattern size
56 cm x 40 cm
6614 x 4724 pixels
at 300 ppi in CMYK

GFT0087
pattern size
60 cm x 55 cm
7087 x 6496 pixels
at 300 ppi in CMYK

page 067 >>

<< page 068

GFT0088
pattern size
74 cm x 50 cm
8740 x 5906 pixels
at 300 ppi in CMYK

GFT0089
pattern size
50 cm x 70 cm
5906 x 8268 pixels
at 300 ppi in CMYK

GFT0090
pattern size
40 cm x 62 cm
4724 x 7323 pixels
at 300 ppi in CMYK

GFT0091
pattern size
pattern size
40 cm x 40 cm
4724 x 4724 pixels
at 300 ppi in CMYK

GFT0092
pattern size
40 cm x 62 cm
4724 x 7323 pixels
at 300 ppi in CMYK

page 071 >>

<< page 072

GFT0093
pattern size
70 cm x 70 cm
8268 x 8268 pixels
at 300 ppi in CMYK

GFT0094
pattern size
60 cm x 55 cm
7087 x 6496 pixels
at 300 ppi in CMYK

GFT0095
pattern size
46 cm x 55 cm
5433 x 6496 pixels
at 300 ppi in CMYK

GFT0096
pattern size
54 cm x 60 cm
6378 x 7087 pixels
at 300 ppi in CMYK

GFT0097
pattern size
30 cm x 30 cm
3543 x 3543 pixels
at 300 ppi in CMYK

GFT0098
pattern size
30 cm x 30 cm
3543 x 3543 pixels
at 300 ppi in CMYK

page 075 >>

<< page 076

GFT0099
pattern size
50 cm x 67 cm
5906 x 7914 pixels
at 300 ppi in CMYK

GFT0100
pattern size
70 cm x 45 cm
8268 x 5315 pixels
at 300 ppi in CMYK

page 077

GFT0101
pattern size
64 cm x 70 cm
7559 x 8268 pixels
at 300 ppi in CMYK

GFT0102
pattern size
pattern size
52 cm x 50 cm
6142 x 5906 pixels
at 300 ppi in CMYK

GFT0103
pattern size
50 cm x 58 cm
5906 x 6850 pixels
at 300 ppi in CMYK

page 079 >>

<< page 080

GFT0104
pattern size
42 cm x 60 cm
4961 x 7087 pixels
at 300 ppi in CMYK

GFT0105
pattern size
42 cm x 60 cm
4961 x 7087 pixels
at 300 ppi in CMYK

GFT0106
pattern size
50 cm x 50 cm
5906 x 5906 pixels
at 300 ppi in CMYK

GFT0107
pattern size
50 cm x 50 cm
5906 x 5906 pixels
at 300 ppi in CMYK

GFT0108
pattern size
pattern size
46 cm x 50 cm
5433 x 5906 pixels
at 300 ppi in CMYK

GFT0109
pattern size
55 cm x 60 cm
6497 x 7087 pixels
at 300 ppi in CMYK

page 083 >>

GFT0110
pattern size
50 cm x 50 cm
5906 x 5906 pixels
at 300 ppi in CMYK

GFT0111
pattern size
44 cm x 55 cm
5197 x 6496 pixels
at 300 ppi in CMYK

GFT0112
pattern size
50 cm x 50 cm
5906 x 5906 pixels
at 300 ppi in CMYK

page 085 >>

GFT0113
pattern size
70 cm x 45 cm
8268 x 5315 pixels
at 300 ppi in CMYK

GFT0114
pattern size
pattern size
50 cm x 60 cm
5906 x 7087 pixels
at 300 ppi in CMYK

GFT0115
pattern size
50 cm x 60 cm
5906 x 7087 pixels
at 300 ppi in CMYK

page 087 >>

<< page 088

GFT0116
pattern size
50 cm x 50 cm
5906 x 5906 pixels
at 300 ppi in CMYK

GFT0117
pattern size
50 cm x 50 cm
5906 x 5906 pixels
at 300 ppi in CMYK

GFT0118
pattern size
50 cm x 47 cm
5906 x 5551 pixels
at 300 ppi in CMYK

GFT0119
pattern size
60 cm x 60 cm
7087 x 7087 pixels
at 300 ppi in CMYK

GFT0120
pattern size
60 cm x 60 cm
7087 x 7087 pixels
at 300 ppi in CMYK

page 091 >>

<< page 092

GFT0121
pattern size
50 cm x 50 cm
5906 x 5906 pixels
at 300 ppi in CMYK

GFT0122
pattern size
58 cm x 50 cm
6851 x 5906 pixels
at 300 ppi in CMYK

GFT0123
pattern size
42 cm x 50 cm
4961 x 5906 pixels
at 300 ppi in CMYK

page 095

GFT0125
pattern size
45 cm x 45 cm
5315 x 5315 pixels
at 300 ppi in CMYK

GFT0126
pattern size
52 cm x 40 cm
6142 x 4724 pixels
at 300 ppi in CMYK

GFT0124
pattern size
52 cm x 40 cm
6142 x 4724 pixels
at 300 ppi in CMYK

<< page 094

<< page 096

GFT0127
pattern size
53 cm x 70 cm
6260 x 8268 pixels
at 300 ppi in CMYK

GFT0128
pattern size
60 cm x 60 cm
7087 x 7087 pixels
at 300 ppi in CMYK

GFT0129
pattern size
50 cm x 55 cm
5906 x 6497 pixels
at 300 ppi in CMYK

GFT0130
pattern size
44 cm x 60 cm
5197 x 7087 pixels
at 300 ppi in CMYK

GFT0131
pattern size
40 cm x 55 cm
4724 x 6496 pixels
at 300 ppi in CMYK

page 099 >>

<< page 100

GFT0132
pattern size
40 cm x 50 cm
4724 x 5906 pixels
at 300 ppi in CMYK

GFT0133
pattern size
40 cm x 50 cm
4724 x 5906 pixels
at 300 ppi in CMYK

GFT0134
pattern size
46 cm x 55 cm
5433 x 6496 pixels
at 300 ppi in CMYK

GFT0135
pattern size
40 cm x 56 cm
4724 x 6614 pixels
at 300 ppi in CMYK

GFT0136
pattern size
40 cm x 56 cm
4724 x 6614 pixels
at 300 ppi in CMYK

GFT0137
pattern size
60 cm x 81 cm
7087 x 9567 pixels
at 300 ppi in CMYK

page 103 >>

<< page 104

GFT0138
pattern size
66 cm x 70 cm
7796 x 8268 pixels
at 300 ppi in CMYK

GFT0139
pattern size
70 cm x 56 cm
8268 x 6615 pixels
at 300 ppi in CMYK

page 105

page 106

GFT0140
pattern size
50 cm x 50 cm
5906 x 5906 pixels
at 300 ppi in CMYK

GFT0141
pattern size
50 cm x 50 cm
5906 x 5906 pixels
at 300 ppi in CMYK

GFT0142
pattern size
42 cm x 60 cm
4961 x 7087 pixels
at 300 ppi in CMYK

page 107 >>

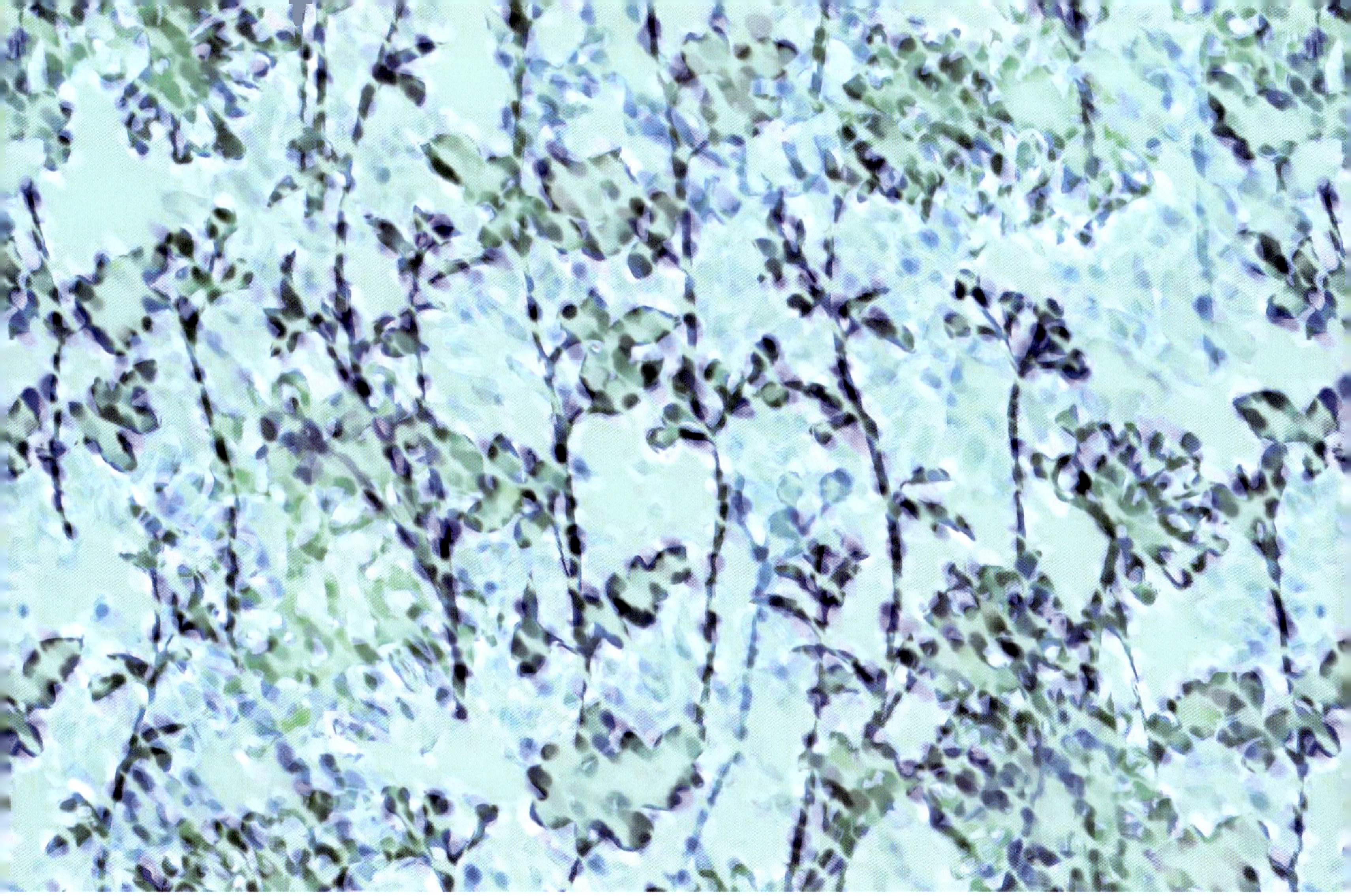

<< page 108

GFT0143
pattern size
40 cm x 53 cm
47241 x 6260 pixels
at 300 ppi in CMYK

GFT0144
pattern size
44 cm x 60 cm
5197 x 7087 pixels
at 300 ppi in CMYK

GFT0145
pattern size
50 cm x 73 cm
5906 x 8622 pixels
at 300 ppi in CMYK

GFT0146
pattern size
60 cm x 43 cm
7087 x 5079 pixels
at 300 ppi in CMYK

GFT0147
pattern size
56 cm x 40 cm
6615 x 4724 pixels
at 300 ppi in CMYK

page 111 >>

GFT0149
pattern size
36 cm x 55 cm
4252 x 6497 pixels
at 300 ppi in CMYK

GFT0150
pattern size
36 cm x 55 cm
4252 x 6497 pixels
at 300 ppi in CMYK

GFT0148
pattern size
60 cm x 55 cm
7087 x 6496 pixels
at 300 ppi in CMYK

<< page 112

page 114

GFT0151
pattern size
50 cm x 50 cm
5906 x 5906 pixels
at 300 ppi in CMYK

GFT0152
pattern size
60 cm x 75 cm
7087 x 8859 pixels
at 300 ppi in CMYK

page 115 >>

<< page 116

GFT0153
pattern size
45 cm x 50 cm
5315 x 5906 pixels
at 300 ppi in CMYK

GFT0154
pattern size
44 cm x 60 cm
5197 x 7087 pixels
at 300 ppi in CMYK

GFT0155
pattern size
55 cm x 70 cm
6497 x 8268 pixels
at 300 ppi in CMYK

page 118

GFT0156
pattern size
54 cm x 60 cm
6378 x 7087 pixels
at 300 ppi in CMYK

GFT0157
pattern size
70 cm x 56 cm
8268 x 6615 pixels
at 300 ppi in CMYK

page 119 >>

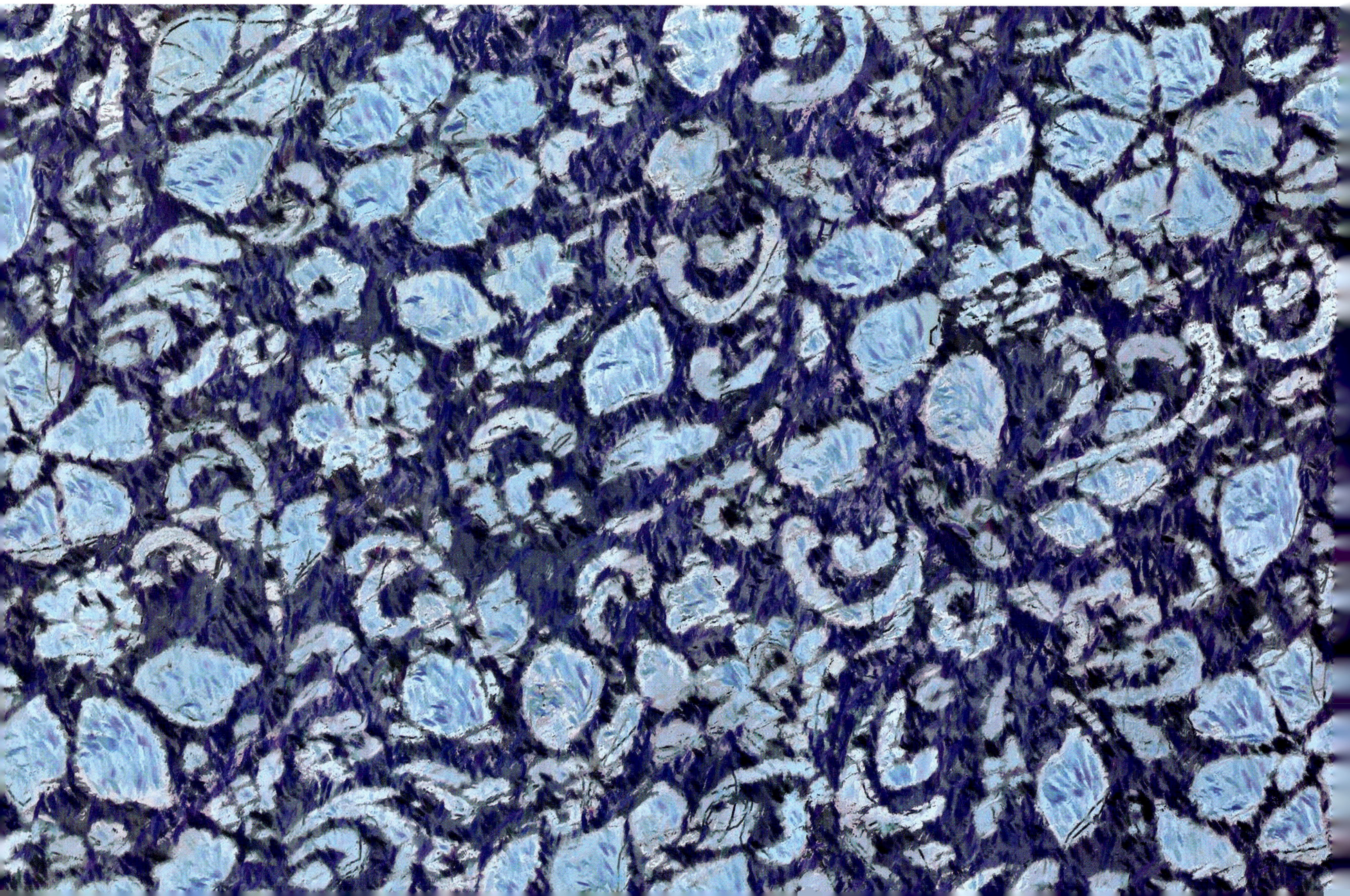

<< page 120

GFT0158
pattern size
50 cm x 58 cm
5906 x 6850 pixels
at 300 ppi in CMYK

GFT0159
pattern size
50 cm x 50 cm
5906 x 5906 pixels
at 300 ppi in CMYK

GFT0160
pattern size
50 cm x 58 cm
5906 x 6850 pixels
at 300 ppi in CMYK

page 121

GFT0161
pattern size
70 cm x 50 cm
8268 x 5906 pixels
at 300 ppi in CMYK

GFT0162
pattern size
50 cm x 70 cm
5906 x 8268 pixels
at 300 ppi in CMYK

page 123 >>

GFT0163
pattern size
50 cm x 70 cm
5906 x 8268 pixels
at 300 ppi in CMYK

GFT0164
pattern size
50 cm x 47 cm
5906 x 5551 pixels
at 300 ppi in CMYK

GFT0165
pattern size
50 cm x 47 cm
5906 x 5551 pixels
at 300 ppi in CMYK

page 125 >>

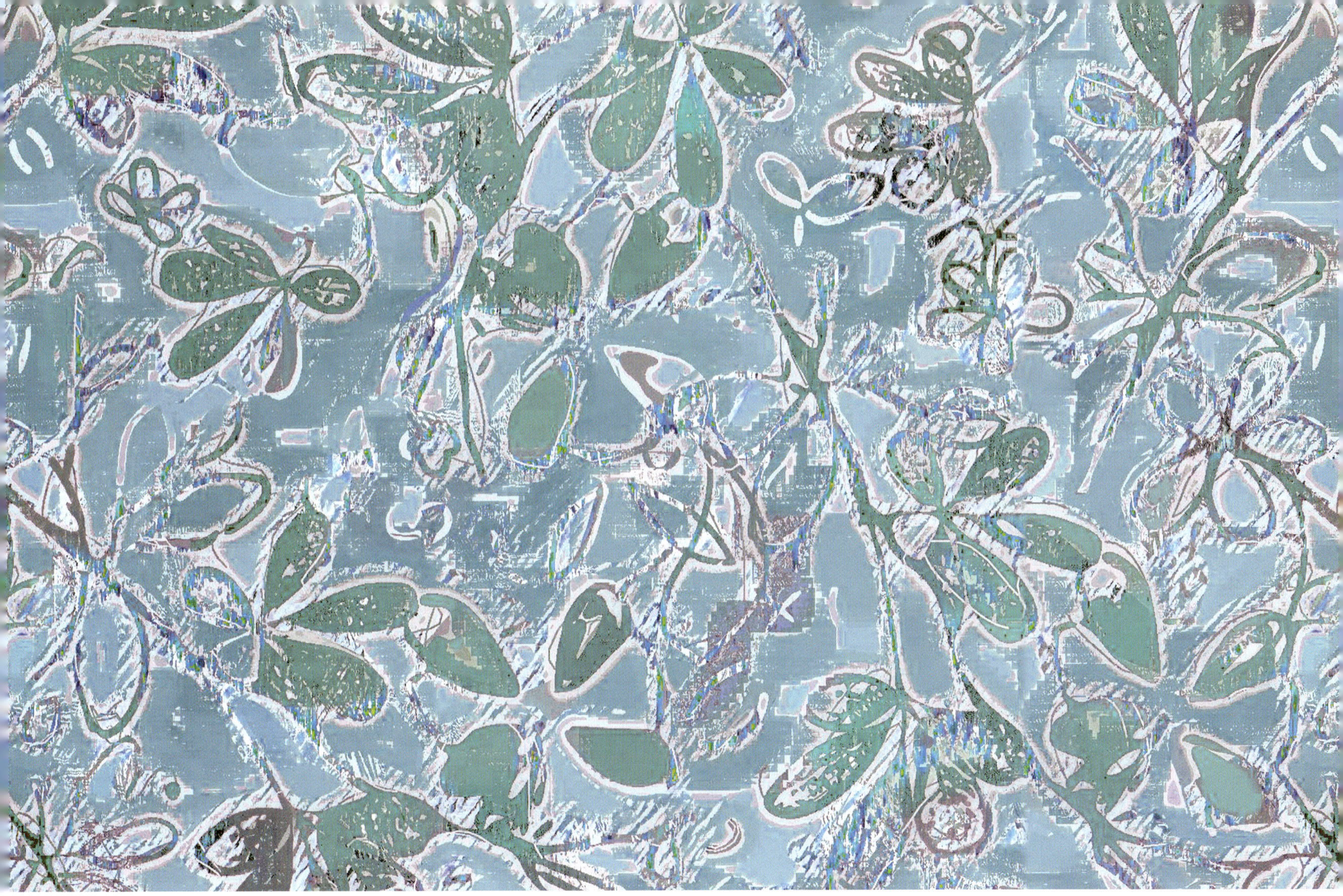

arkivia books collection

WHY ARKIVIA BOOKS?

For those who work as stylists or designers of product lines in various merceological sectors, one of the most important jobs is to determine the look that the line should have to attract clients and distinguish itself from others.

Research is fundamental, before any design can be made, research using books, magazines, samples of objects found all over the world. This results in a large quantity of ideas on which the marketing department works before starting to develop one of them.
A long and expensive process to reach the development of the designs, keeping in mind the production methods.

I have inserted into my books this kind of know-how:

1 - Research into a tendency theme
2 - Development of creative ideas that illustrate it
3 - Professional artworks for immediate production with
- that look.

WHO FINDS ARKIVIA BOOKS USEFUL?

1 - Those who create products every day and need to - -
- document a single theme suitable to the product.
2 - Companies that with a small amount of money, very
- low compared with the high costs of creative studios, --
- can access material ready to be used and developed
- by their internal staff.

In the recent past, Tendency Books have been produced for a restricted club of professional people who could afford the high cost of this sort of book (around 1000/1500 euros).
I have decided to create books with the same spirit but within the reach of any professional in image.
As expensive as a good quality book but no more than is accepted in bookshops.

SOME TECHNICAL INFORMATION

All files in the CD or in DVD are in hi-res format: PHOTOSHOP PDF format for bitmap files or ILLUSTRATOR format for vector files, accessible by all programmes and compatible with WINDOWS and MAC.

All vectorial files are modifiable because they are the original graphics and the material is produced in a professional way and ready to use.

The designs are free to be used by those who buy the books in accordance with copyright terms present in each book.

Tecno Pop Textures vol.1

ISBN 9788888766010
HARDBACK • 144 pages
size 24cm x 30.7cm
200 TEXTURES saved
in 4 ways 800 files in all

2 Free CDs included
for WINDOWS and MAC
Vector and Bitmap Files
Ready for Production.
The use is Free

200 textures in the new POP style, using simple and geometric shapes. This collection is intended for textile fabrics in clothing and home furniture. But also some designs are suitable for wrapping and wallpaper or for stationery, packaging and accessory collections.

Optical Textures vol.1

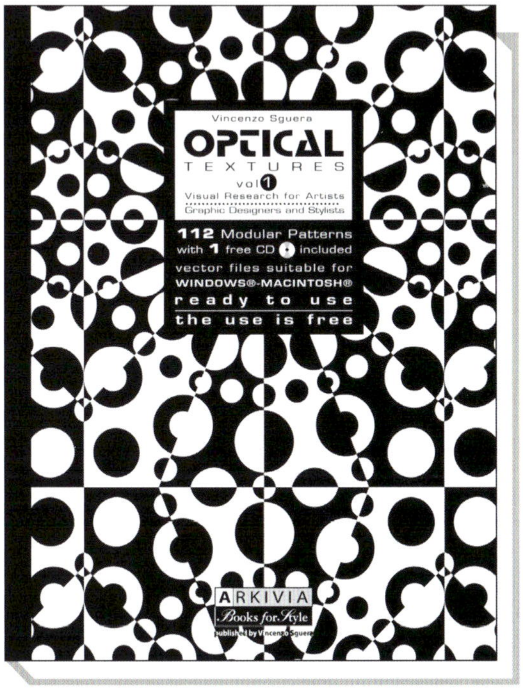

ISBN 9788888766027
PAPERBACK • 128 pages
size 24cm x 30.7cm
112 TEXTURES saved
in 4 ways-448 files in all

1 Free CD included
for WINDOWS and MAC
Vector and Bitmap Files
Ready for Production.
The use is Free

This book develops ideas inspired by "OP ART" The most part of these textures is based on tricks of visual perception: using rules of perspective to give the illusion of three-dimensional space. Op art works are usually abstract, with many of the better known pieces made in only black and white.

Styling Book vol.1

ISBN 9788888766034 HARDBACK Edition
ISBN 9788888766515 PAPERBACK Edition
144 pages) • size 24cm x 30.7cm
229 MODEL SHEETS • plus PRINTS, TEXTURES
2 CDs or 1 DVD included for WINDOWS and MAC.
Vector Files • The use is Free.

The 16 families of characters have been developed all in a fresh and modern style. Real model sheets can be used for graphic needs.

You can move parts of them to create other positions since they are created in Adobe Illustrator with separable parts (body, arms, head, eyes etc).

Junior Pop Textures vol.1

ISBN 9788888766041 HARDBACK Edition
ISBN 9788888766522 PAPERBACK Edition
144 pages • size 24cm x 30.7cm
200 TEXTURES saved in 2 ways-400 files in all.
I Free CD included for WINDOWS and MAC.
Vector Files • The use is Free.

This book develops textures in the new POP Style. Textures for kids and teenagers, using characters and shapes, simple and geometric.

Designs useful for textile fabrics, for clothing and home furniture, wall and gift papers, gadgets and stationery items.

Styling Book vol.2

ISBN 9788888766058 HARDBACK Edition
ISBN 9788888766539 PAPERBACK Edition
160 pages • size 24cm x 30.7cm
More than 500 designs with 1 DVD included
Vector Files • The use is Free.

The 16 families of characters have been developed all in a fresh and modern style. Real model sheets can be used for graphic needs.

You can move parts of them to create other positions since they are created in Adobe Illustrator with separable parts (body, arms, head, eyes etc).

New Age Textures vol.1

ISBN 9788888766003 HARDBACK Edition
ISBN 9788888766065 PAPERBACK Edition
144 pages) • size 24cm x 30.7cm
423 TEXTURES saved for WINDOWS and MAC
3 CDs or 1 DVD with EPS Bitmap Files (300 dpi).
CMYK-300 dpi resolution • The use is Free.

This book develops ideas inspired by the "New Age style" where Nature plays a large part. The use is free and the 423 Textures are contained in 1 DVD easy to consult following the book.

It reproduces all the designs in natural format, indicates the full development of the module and the textures are already set to be repeated to infinity in perfect alignment.

Gothic Pop Textures vol.1

ISBN 9788888766072 HARDBACK Edition
ISBN 9788888766546 PAPERBACK Edition
144 pages • size 24cm x 30.7cm
130 TEXTURES saved in 4 ways-520 files in all.
I Free DVD included for WINDOWS and MAC.
Vector and Bitmap Files • The use is Free.

This book develops textures in the new GOTHIC taste. From the Neo Floreal and Liberty Style, soft-coloured or black and white textures.

Designs useful for textile fabrics,for clothing and home furniture, wall and gift papers, gadgets and stationery items.

Gothic Pop Textures vol.2

ISBN 9788888766089
HARDBACK • 144 pages
size 24cm x 30.7cm
130 TEXTURES saved
in 5 ways-650 files in all

1 Free DVD included
for WINDOWS and MAC
Vector and Bitmap Files
Ready for Production.
The use is Free

This second volume develops further designs in neo-gothic style. It too is inspired by modern and floral liberty, but with the accent on pop: less elegant, but fresh and younger. More contaminations of various styles, colors and more creative freedom.

Character Styling vol.1-the Cat

ISBN 9788888766096
HARDBACK • 72 pages
size 24cm x 30.7cm
149 MODEL SHEETS
54 PRINTS
14 TEXTURES

1 Free CD included
for WINDOWS and MAC
Vector and Bitmap Files
Ready for Production.
The use is Free

This BOOK, the first of a new series has an ambitious objective: to develop new characters and to teach how to create them.

Each title will develop one theme at a time but with different ways of characterizing them. I will show how to construct the basic forms.

Gothic Pop Graphics vol.1

ISBN 9788888766102
HARDBACK • 144 pages
size 24cm x 30.7cm
132 GRAPHICS in 3 color variations saved in 5 ways
1980 files in all

1 Free DVD included
for WINDOWS and MAC
Vector and Bitmap Files
Ready for Production.
The use is Free

Prints and Logos for all sorts of use, in the style that characterizes the "ten years style" of the century.

A flow of creativity in counterpoint to the past from which it freely culls elements in a fluid and artistic way.

Natural Pop Textures vol.1

ISBN 9788888766119 HARDBACK Edition
ISBN 9788888766553 PAPERBACK Edition
144 pages • size 24cm x 30.7cm
130 TEXTURES saved in 5 ways - 650 files in all.
I Free DVD included for WINDOWS and MAC.
Vector and BitmapFiles • The use is Free.

130 elegant textures, composed with a light touch and grace. A breath of natural modernity, with their concise and linear signs.

Delicate, tonal colours that can be used from clothing to interior decorating, from accessories to wallpapering.

Natural Pop Graphics vol.1

ISBN 9788888766126 HARDBACK Edition
ISBN 9788888766560 PAPERBACK Edition
144 pages • size 24cm x 30.7cm
205 GRAPHICS saved in 5 ways - 1025 files in all.
I Free DVD included for WINDOWS and MAC.
Vector and BitmapFiles • The use is Free.

Prints and Logos for all sorts of use, with a light touch and grace. A breath of natural modernity.

All the designs are vectorial. They can be used with many graphic softwares, such as ILLUSTRATOR.

Character Styling vol.2-the Bear

ISBN 9788888766133
HARDBACK • 72 pages
size 24cm x 30.7cm
146 MODEL SHEETS
61 PRINTS
15 TEXTURES

1 Free CD included
for WINDOWS and MAC
Vector and Bitmap Files
Ready for Production.
The use is Free

This BOOK is the 2nd of this series and I have increased the numbers of Characters to 8. I wanted to develop more Character ideas to offer a wider choice of use and style. For each one I will show how to construct the basic forms, the psychological and chromatic characteristics.

Black & White Matrix 1

ISBN 9788888766140 HARDBACK Edition
ISBN 9788888766577 PAPERBACK Edition
144 pages • size 24cm x 30.7cm
325 TEXTURES saved in 5 ways - 1625 files in all.
I Free DVD included for WINDOWS and MAC.
Vector and BitmapFiles • The use is Free.

A symphony of BLACK and WHITE, unending geometries in a mosiac full of structures as fabrics are, to satisfy our need for B&W.

325 vectorial designs where the development of one generates others in an explosion of ideas ready and available for free use.

Matrix Graphix 1

ISBN 9788888766157
HARDBACK • 144 pages
size 24cm x 30.7cm
250 GRAPHICS saved
in 5 ways 1250 files in all.

1 Free DVD included
for WINDOWS and MAC
Vector and Bitmap Files
Ready for Production.
The use is Free

The spirit of the time and the memory of the fizzy 80's have produced a miracle of sorts: a synthetical look with one color for each graphic.

More life and passion, a flow of strong flavours, with ideas that speak of yesterday but of tomorrow, too.

Black & White Matrix 2

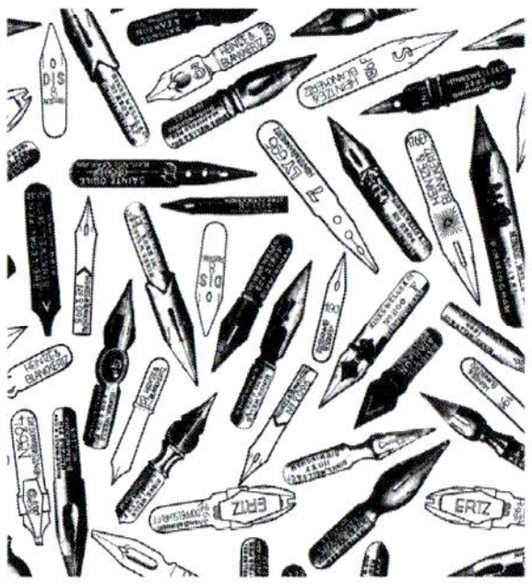

ISBN 9788888766164 HARDBACK Edition
ISBN 9788888766584 PAPERBACK Edition
144 pages • size 24cm x 30.7cm
275 TEXTURES saved in 5 ways - 1375 files in all.
I Free DVD included for WINDOWS and MAC.
Vector and BitmapFiles • The use is Free.

This time, the colours of black are tinged with things, objects, people, animals, all scattered and overlapping to generate a modern style of textures

A brushstroke of freshness, no half-tones, lines, silhouettes or synthetic images develop single themes, entering by right into the world of decoration.

Teen Girl Graphics Vol.1

ISBN 9788888766171 HARDBACK Edition
ISBN 9788888766591 PAPERBACK Edition
96 pages • size 24cm x 30.7cm
200 GRAPHICS saved in 5 ways - 1000 files in all.
I Free DVD included for WINDOWS and MAC.
Vector and BitmapFiles.

This book is the first of a series dedicated to Stylistic Studios which have produced so much creativity, applied to the market and used by countless firms.This project stems from a studio with many years of experience which has agreed to make public its fantastic work.

Ultra Pop Textures vol.1

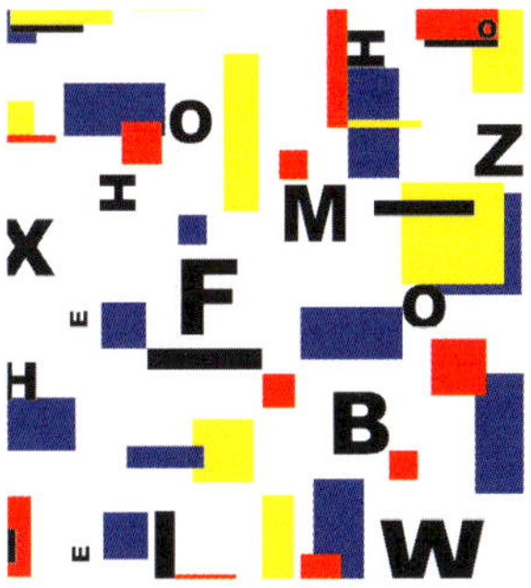

ISBN 9788888766188
HARDBACK • 144 pages
size 24cm x 30.7cm
250 TEXTURES saved
in 5 ways-1250 files in all

1 Free DVD included
for WINDOWS and MAC
Vector and Bitmap Files
Ready for Production.
The use is Free

The essence of the eighties, strong and varied, is the mix. Even in a provocative way in order to find new roads, roads that have signposted the present time, such as the Postmodern Look in contraposition to the elegant Minimalism of HI-TECH or Optical matched with Floreal, geometries and chaotic puzzles.

Ultra Pop Graphics vol.1

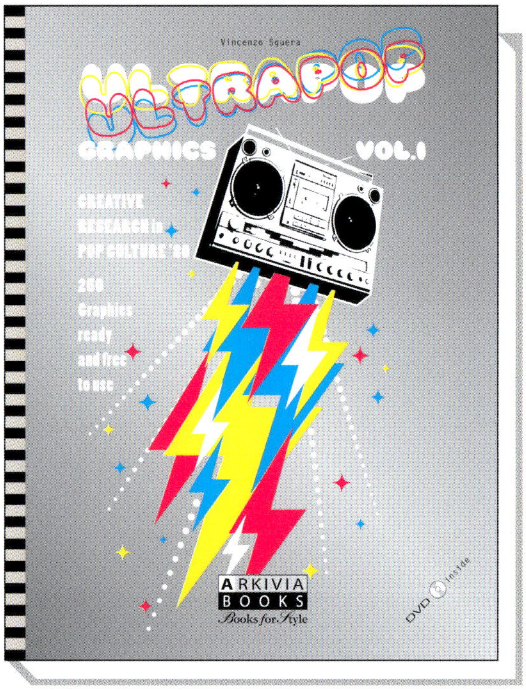

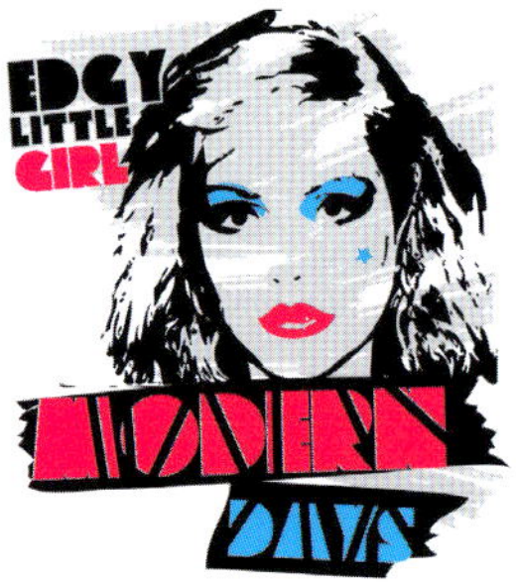

ISBN 9788888766195
HARDBACK • 144 pages
size 24cm x 30.7cm
250 GRAPHICS saved in
5 ways - 1250 files in all.

1 Free DVD included
for WINDOWS and MAC
Vector and Bitmap Files
Ready for Production.
The use is Free

The essence of the eighties, strong and varied, is the mix. Even in a provocative way in order to find new roads, roads that have signposted the present time, such as the Postmodern Look in contraposition to the elegant Minimalism of HI-TECH or Optical matched with Floreal, geometries and chaotic puzzles.

Junior Pop Graphics Vol.1

ISBN 9788888766201
HARDBACK • 96 pages
size 24cm x 30.7cm
213 TEXTURES saved
in 5 ways-1065 files in all

1 Free DVD included
for WINDOWS and MAC
Vector and Bitmap Files
Ready for Production.
The use is Free

Graphics for children that portray our world in a happy way, without dramatization and full of joy and delight.

On every page a Unique Brand, a strong idea to depart from and as we know, for a creative person, the world of children is a journey without end.

Ethno Pop Textures Vol.1

ISBN 9788888766218
HARDBACK • 112 pages
size 24cm x 30.7cm
100 TEXTURES saved
in 5 ways 500 files in all.

1 Free CD included
for WINDOWS and MAC
Vector and Bitmap Files
Ready for Production.
The use is Free

In an increasingly globalized world, creativity is becoming more and more a common heritage. Research in fashion has always drawn from cultures all over the world, reproposing for itself designs from ethnic groups which are far away in time and space.

Teen Boy Graphics vol.1

ISBN 9788888766225
HARDBACK • 96 pages
size 24cm x 30.7cm
200 GRAPHICS saved
in 4 ways-800 files in all

1 Free DVD included
for WINDOWS and MAC
Vector and Bitmap Files.

This book is the second of a series dedicated to Stylistic Studios which have produced so much creativity, applied to the market and used by countless firms.This project stems from a studio with many years of experience which has agreed to make public its fantastic work.

Ultra Pop Textures Vol.2

ISBN 9788888766232
HARDBACK • 144 pages
size 24cm x 30.7cm
120 TEXTURES saved
in 5 ways 600 files in all.

1 Free CD included
for WINDOWS and MAC
Vector and Bitmap Files
Ready for Production.
The use is Free

These designs describe a path which covers 3 decades from the 60's to the 80's. They highlight a very special decorative taste, at the same time refined and naif, floral and geometric in unison. Designs that communicate the rhythm of an epoch full of colours and elegance.

Grunge Textures vol.1

ISBN 9788888766249
PAPERBACK • 144 pages
size 24cm x 30.7cm
160 TEXTURES saved
in 5 ways-800 files in all

1 Free DVD included
for WINDOWS and MAC
Vector and Bitmap Files
Ready for Production.
The use is Free

"Grunge", a term intended to indicate something disorderly, casual or ruined.
The uses of this book are many, in decoration or to give a different touch to the image, creating movement where necessary.
At the same time it is a tendency book and also a very useful source book

Logopop Volume1

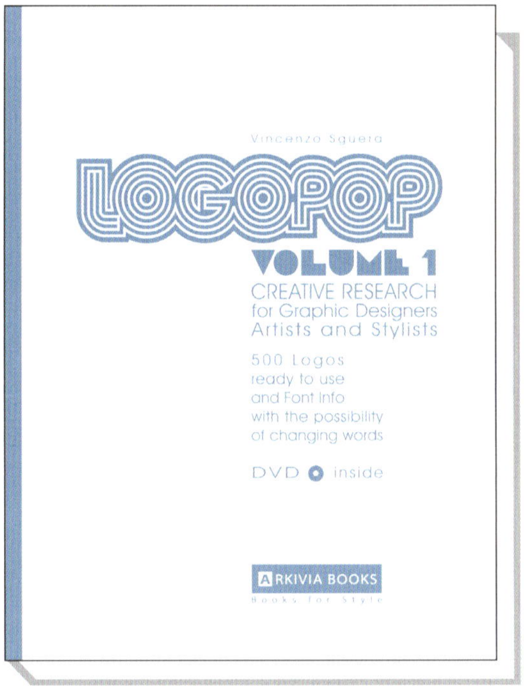

ISBN 9788888766256
HARDBACK • 160 pages
size 24cm x 30.7cm
500 LOGOS saved in 5 ways - 2500 files in all.

1 Free DVD included
for WINDOWS and MAC
Vector and Bitmap Files
Ready for Production.
The use is Free

500 Logos ready to use and font info with the possibility of changing all the words to personalize your graphics and make your own Logo!

In the panorama of books which offer thousands of Logos there has always been a lack of one with new and original designs and with the permission to use.

Ethno Pop Textures vol.2

ISBN 9788888766263
HARDBACK • 112 pages
size 24cm x 30.7cm
100 TEXTURES saved in 5 ways-500 files in all

1 Free DVD included
for WINDOWS and MAC
Vector and Bitmap Files
Ready for Production.
The use is Free

In an increasingly globalized world, creativity is becoming more and more a common heritage. Research in fashion has always drawn from cultures all over the world, reproposing for itself designs from ethnic groups which are far away in time and space.

Natural Pop Textures Vol.2

ISBN 9788888766270
HARDBACK • 144 pages
size 24cm x 30.7cm
122 TEXTURES saved
in 5 ways 610 files in all.

1 Free DVD included
for WINDOWS and MAC
Vector and Bitmap Files
Ready for Production.
The use is Free

This second book develops more soft and elegant designs inspired by modern North-European Design also called Scandinavian Style.

New ideas in delicate colours and graphic synthesis, clean and essential, suitable for home decoration, interior design and fashion clothing textiles.

Kinetic Art Textures vol.1

ISBN 9788888766287
HARDBACK • 144 pages
size 24cm x 30.7cm
120 TEXTURES saved
in 5 ways-600 files in all

1 Free DVD included
for WINDOWS and MAC
Vector and Bitmap Files
Ready for Production.
The use is Free

Beyond the image and the meaning in every work, there are rhythm and structure to catch the aesthetics abstracted from the meaning.

The geometries have their own values apart from what they represent and they do so in a continuous and rhythmic way. This style is "KINETIC ART".

Animal Style Textures Vol.1

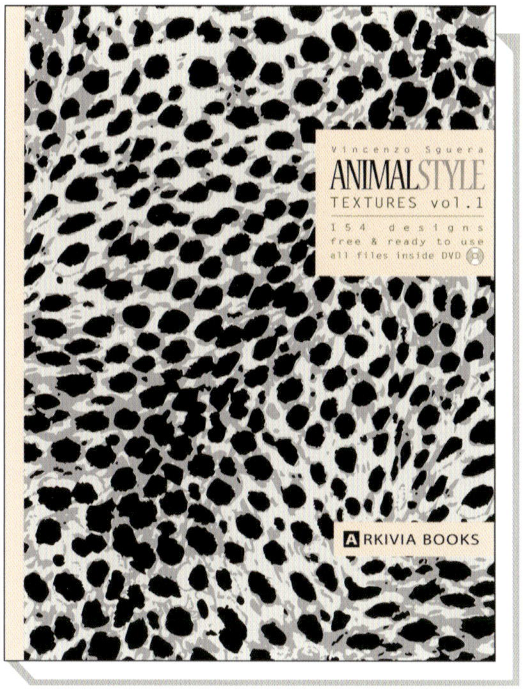

ISBN 9788888766294
HARDBACK • 160 pages
size 24cm x 30.7cm
154 TEXTURES saved
in 5 ways 770 files in all.

1 Free DVD included
for WINDOWS and MAC
Vector and Bitmap Files
Ready for Production.
The use is Free

There is a tendency that has slowly but surely imposed itself: the style inspired by animal skins. Strong, essential and recognizable it has managed to renew itself, passing from a simple proposal of natural skins to mixing these in a fresh and new way.

Flower Fashion Textures vol.1

ISBN 9788888766300
HARDBACK • 144 pages
size 24cm x 30.7cm
300 TEXTURES saved
in 5 ways-1500 files in all

1 Free DVD included
for WINDOWS and MAC
Vector and Bitmap Files
Ready for Production.
The use is Free

The world of Fashion has always drawn inspiration from nature, colors and decorations. Small and large flowers with stripes and squares or provençal designs. Roses and violets, poppies and daisies in a continuous flow of textures, making vectorial and synthetic designs following the trend of present graphics.

Black and White Matrix 3

ISBN 9788888766317
HARDBACK • 144 pages
size 24cm x 30.7cm
250 TEXTURES saved
in 5 ways 1250 files in all.

1 Free DVD included
for WINDOWS and MAC
Vector and Bitmap Files
Ready for Production.
The use is Free

When decorative cultures from far away places meet. Europe and Asia with their traditions may coexist and adopt a mature look.

Various decorative layers rich in detail, lead beyond the level of taste bringing a more graphic and essential pot pourri.

Geometric Textures for Fashion vol.1

ISBN 9788888766324
HARDBACK • 144 pages
size 24cm x 30.7cm
480 TEXTURES saved
in 5 ways+106 palettes

1 Free DVD included
for WINDOWS and MAC
Vector and Bitmap Files
Ready for Production.
The use is Free

This book offers vector designs of geometric fabrics, simple or structured with some elements in the Victorian or Liberty style, and with an emphasis on combinations of minimalist designs, which are useful for furniture and fashion. The designs are divided into groups, coordinated together and harmonized each with the same colour palette.

Abstract Textures vol.1

ISBN 9788888766331
HARDBACK • 160 pages
size 24cm x 30.7cm
200 TEXTURES saved
JPG 300 ppi / JPG 72 ppi.

1 Free DVD included
for WINDOWS and MAC
Bitmap Modular Files
Ready for Production.
The use is Free

Abstract is real, as an idea, representing a world so vague, undefinable but equally real was the challenge for artists who wanted to break free from the shackles of codified reality.

Entering into abstractionism reveals new form and beauty, where the rules of yesterday no longer apply to create others, transcend old visual cultures and generate new ones.

Simple Nature Textures vol.1

ISBN 9788888766348
HARDBACK • 144 pages
size 24cm x 30.7cm
123 TEXTURES saved
in 5 ways / 615 files

1 Free DVD included
for WINDOWS and MAC
Vector and Bitmap Files
Ready for Production.
The use is Free

Flowers are never enough, if they are in soft, pastel tones, as if drawn on a sketch pad.
Nature is a breath, a caress that covers you, interwoven leaves, flights of birds or dragonflies.

Suitable for timeless fabrics, collections that have the fragrance of spring, of a past time which we want to return.
Nature is tinged with nostalgia and becomes simple..

Ethno Pop Textures - Black Edition

ISBN 9788888766393
HARDBACK • 144 pages
size 24cm x 30.7cm
200 TEXTURES saved in
5 ways -1000 files in all.

1 Free DVD included
for WINDOWS and MAC
Bitmap Modular Files
Ready for Production.
The use is Free

The charm of ethnic designs increases considerably if interpreted in Black & White. While taking away the magic of colours, typical of these designs, this gives them an added chance for greater use. In fact, the graphical structure of these designs is suitable for all circumstances and so they become casual and elegant at the same time.

Liberty Style Textures vol.1

Available from September 2015

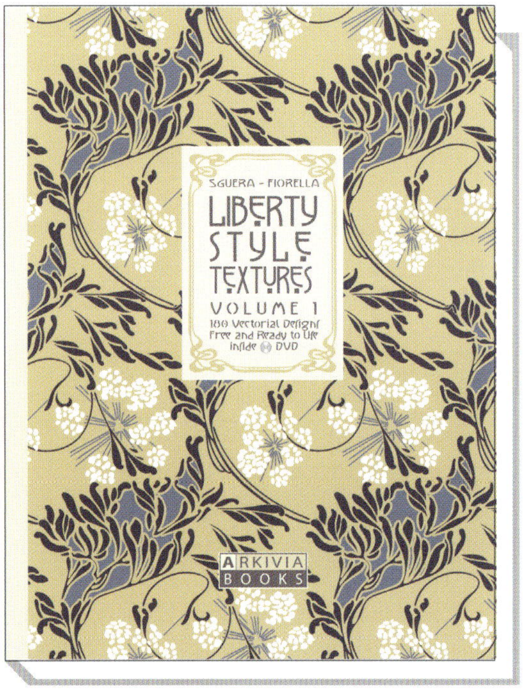

ISBN 9788888766362
HARDBACK • 144 pages
size 24cm x 30.7cm
180 TEXTURES saved in
5 ways -900 files in all.

1 Free DVD included
for WINDOWS and MAC
Vector and Bitmap Files
Ready for Production.
The use is Free

The Liberty Style or Art Nouveau has developed designs that have remained as art and decoration for their remarkable peculiarities: geometry and nature together. Features are the organic forms, curved lines, with ornaments made essentially of plants or flowers to decorate anything from home décor to clothing.